P9-DFC-537

A GUIDE FOR PARENTS & EDUCATORS

When Kids Say *NO* to School

Helping Children at Risk of Failure, Refusal, or Dropping Out

Elaine K. McEwan

Harold Shaw Publishers
Wheaton, Illinois

ISBN 0-87788-406-4

Cover design by David LaPlaca

Library of Congress Cataloging-in-Publication Data

McEwan, Elaine K., 1941-
    When kids say no to school : helping children at risk of failure,
    refusal, or dropping out / by Elaine K. McEwan.
        p.   cm.
    Includes bibliographical references.
    ISBN 0-87788-406-4
    1. School phobia. 2. Home and school. I. Title.
    LB1091.M43 1998
    370.15'8—dc21   98-23002
                                                                    CIP

---

03 02 01 00 99 98

10 9 8 7 6 5 4 3 2 1

Contents

*Please note that names used here to refer to real people have
been changed to protect their privacy.*

96099

Introduction

Take one sensitive and intelligent second-grader. Add a two-week absence from school due to strep throat. Mix in a frantic mother, a crowded school with poor discipline, and a teacher with thirty-five students. Stir well. What do you get? A child who suddenly decides he won't go to school . . . school stress.

Take one fifth-grader with poor grades and low self-esteem. Add a teacher who loves power and control. Mix in a pinch of hyperactivity and a cup of learning disabilities and let cool. What's the result? A child who hates school with a passion . . . school stress.

Take one high school student with sporadic attendance. Mix in a bad attitude and some alcohol. Add a high school with a gang problem and sprinkle with depression and a recent divorce. Simmer until it boils over. What do you have? A high school dropout . . . school stress.

These recipes are a parent's worst nightmare—a child who refuses to go to school, one who hates school, or one who just plain drops out. I have experienced this nightmare—what I've come to call *school stress*—from every angle: as a teacher, as a parent, and as a principal.

Unfortunately, I received no training to deal with school stress in my administrative coursework. But I learned fast on the job; dealing with kids who exhibited every symptom of school stress in the book was a part of nearly every day. Crying kindergartners, hypo-chondriacal second-graders, and truant sixth-grad-ers—I've seen them all. I've chauffeured stubborn school-refusers who had to be coaxed out of their paja-mas so I could drive them to school. I've tracked down tough truants in their neighborhood hideouts. Along the way I've worked with countless numbers of frus-trated families, and together we've developed plans for getting their reluctant learners back into the class-room. If your child hates school and can't or won't go, there's help for you in the pages ahead.

Chapter 1 will give you a brief overview of the prob-lem. You'll learn some things that might surprise you about why kids refuse to go to school. Chapter 2 con-tains the School Stress Diagnostic Checklist that will help you pinpoint the particular reasons your child doesn't want to be in school. Chapter 3 offers specific solutions to your family's problem. Chapter 4 provides fifty ideas for eliminating school stress in your child's life. In chapter 5 we'll look at some steps to take if you're not getting the help you need from school per-sonnel. And finally, in chapter 6, you'll find dozens of activities that will help you take a proactive approach to raising a confident, stress-free learner.

1
Why Do Kids Refuse to Go?

When I was a brand-new teacher, I tried not to take it personally when Tommy stopped coming to my fifth-grade classroom. He complained of severe stomachaches, and his parents said school was giving him an ulcer. I don't know who was more traumatized by this experience, Tommy or I. Tommy eventually came back, and we finished the school year with flying colors, but more than thirty years later, I still remember him.

My second experience with school refusal hit a little closer to home. My son, Patrick, announced one morning that he wasn't going to kindergarten that afternoon. He could give me no reason for his decision, but the set of his jaw told me he was serious. "You have to go; it's your job," I explained. I had a new part-time job and would be going off to work myself. "I can't," he countered. We discussed the issue heatedly for most of

the morning and reached a stalemate on the steps of
the school as the final bell rang. He held his ground
and I was a wimp. He went to work with me that
afternoon and certainly had more fun than I did. My
colleagues treated him to soda and cookies, and he
read books and watched videos while I worked. Mi-
raculously, when time for school rolled around the next
day, he said nothing about accompanying me to work,
his apparent curiosity about how I was spending my
afternoons satisfied. I breathed a giant sigh of relief.

The Problem

Psychologists and psychiatrists who study the problem
of why kids like Tommy and Patrick can't or won't go to
school have had a hard time coming up with a precise
label for this behavior. The most common term for it
has been *school phobia*. But it's also been called school
refusal behavior, nonattendance at school, separation
anxiety, acute school-induced anxiety, retreat neurosis,
and school avoidance. The condition was first described
in the 1930s, when kids who wouldn't go to school were
thought to have a personality disorder characterized
by a deep-seated obsessional neurosis. And who was
the cause? Unfortunately, those who studied the problem blamed Mom.

But we've learned a lot since then about why kids
won't or can't go to school and now realize that—in
addition to family dynamics—a child's temperament
and personality, the school experience itself, and the
pressures of family and community life at the close of

the twentieth century are generating a whole new set of explanations for why kids won't go to school. For that reason, I've chosen to put a new, more general label on the grab-bag of school-refusal symptoms that plague parents, educators, and mental health professionals—*school stress*. School stress is the subject of study by researchers around the world. The phenomenon is on the rise in Japan, where the extremely competitive academic atmosphere is resulting in more and more Japanese young people saying "no" to school. And the problem has been described in both European and South American countries as well. Between 2 and 3 percent of American school-age children have documented episodes of school stress during their learning careers, and many more such episodes go unreported and unresolved. But there are solutions to the problem, as you will discover in the pages ahead.

Who Are These Refusers and Why Won't They Go?

Who are the kids who can't or won't go to school? The researchers and experts in the field of school phobia describe it this way. A school phobic is one who has:

- a severe difficulty in attending school, often amounting to prolonged absence;
- severe emotional distress, shown by such symptoms as excessive fearfulness, undue tempers, and complaints of feeling ill without obvious organic cause; and

- a habit of staying at home—with the knowledge of the parents—when he or she should be at school.[1]

Another researcher defines it this way:

[School phobia] often starts with vague complaints of school or reluctance to attend, progressing to total refusal to go to school or to remain in school in the face of persuasion, entreaty, recrimination and punishment by parents and pressure from teachers, family doctors, and truant officers. The behavior may be accompanied by overt signs of anxiety or even panic when the time comes to go to school and most children cannot even leave home to set out for school. Many who do, return home half-way there and some children, once at school, rush home in a state of anxiety. Many children insist that they want to go to school and are prepared to do so but cannot manage it when the time comes.[2]

While these definitions certainly describe the classic cases of school phobia mentioned in the research journals, they don't begin to cover either the range of school stress problems I've experienced as an educator or the different ways these problems are manifested. I've identified more than a dozen ways in which school stress is manifested.

Kindergarten No-shows
The first category of school refusers is made up of kids who are heading off to school for the first time. These

less-than-eager learners are required to leave the security of home (or another comfortable setting) for a
brand-new ball game. They cling to their mothers, all
the while sobbing pathetically, their separation anxiety palpable. One can't help but sympathize with these
terror-stricken tots. They're afraid Mom (or Dad) is
leaving them for good, and they'll go to any lengths to
keep from being deserted. I've personally witnessed
more than my share of knock-down, drag-out, sit-down
strikes at the kindergarten classroom door in my
school. Even if someone manages to get this child in
the door, she may spend most of her school day alter-
nately sobbing, worrying about Mom, or desperately
clinging to the teacher.

The Princess (or the Prince) and the Pea: Imaginary School Stressors

Sensitive, intelligent kids with overactive imaginations
can find plenty of "possible" or "probable" traumas at
school to cause worry, fear, or anxiety. Much like the
proverbial fairy-tale princess who could feel the irritat-
ing pea no matter how many mattresses were stacked
upon it, the hypersensitive child will find the irritant in
his or her environment and fixate on it. Even the mere
possibility of failing a test, being teased or picked last,
not knowing the right answer when called on, or being
reprimanded by the teacher is enough to strike terror in
the heart of the hyper-sensitive student.

Most kids can cope with these scenarios when they
do occur, but for some children, the remotest likelihood
for disaster is enough reason to pull up the covers and

face the wall. Overanxious children tend to be perfectionists who want to be first and best in everything. At the slightest hint of frustration or failure, they become tense, nervous, and anxious and try to figure out ways to flee from the situation.

Post-traumatic Stress Syndrome

This term has been used to describe a whole range of symptoms that adults can experience after going through a particularly traumatic event in their lives. When kids experience tragedies like death, divorce, or serious illness, they also can suffer from this syndrome, and one of the fallouts in their young lives can be severe school stress. Unable to bounce back from a major change or loss, their post-traumatic stress shows itself in a debilitating inability to attend school. Traumas that kids might experience include, but are not limited to, an accident or illness; a new baby on the scene; loss of employment by a parent; divorce or separation of parents; death of a sibling, parent, or close family member; alcoholism or parental abuse; moving to a new house (even if the school doesn't change); or loss of a school friend through moving or death.

Danger Ahead: Real-life Stressors at School

The school experience itself is fraught with plenty of possibilities for stress that are all-too-real. Playground bullies, cruel teachers, and tough competition are just a few of the reasons kids give for wanting to stay home. And these are the easy ones. Violence, property crimes, abuse, and sexual harassment are not uncommon experiences for many of today's students. A recent *U.S. News and World Report* article on school violence reported that more than three million crimes are committed in or near the eighty-five thousand public schools of our nation. Consider these statistics:

- 2.4 million students have personal property stolen at school;
- 112,000 students are robbed at school through force, a show of weapons, or threats;
- 282,000 students are physically attacked at school;
- 800,000 students stay home because they are afraid to go to school.

It doesn't take much imagination to figure out why a child wouldn't want to go to school faced with possibilities like these. And even the accepted aspects of schooling like academic pressure and competition can be very real stressors for the serious student. Leave aside the fictionalized view of those "good old golden rule days" as carefree and fun, and consider a more accurate picture of what schools are really about: crowds, praise, and power.[3]

Crowds, Competition, and Control: Everyday Challenges

Everything that's done in school is done in a crowd, and rarely does a student have anything to say about where and when his crowd is herded along to the next activity or location. In addition, kids are constantly being sized up and sorted out. Succeeding in school is often about garnering the praise of the teacher and living with the constant pressure of being evaluated. If you're a Buzzard instead of a Bluebird, imagine the stress.

Stress in the classroom is also caused by power—and the people who wield it. Whether you get a drink, go to the restroom, stand up, or sit down, it is at the teacher's discretion. The teacher is the commanding general, and the student is the foot soldier. As a principal, I took my responsibility to make school a more humane place very seriously. I tried to build freedom, choice, and fun into our school program. I had lunch every day with a different group of students and listened to what they told me about our school environment and then took steps to remedy problems. And, most importantly, I tried to hire teachers who were empathetic, caring people in addition to being effective instructors. Now I preach the importance of a caring school climate to other administrators. But too many schools remain intimidating, hazardous environments.

In addition to the crowds, praise, and power that characterize school life, consider four other aspects of classroom life that are pervasive: delay, denial, interruption, and social distraction. Children who are impatient, impulsive, and easily distracted seem destined for failure in such a system.

True School Phobia
True school phobia is a neurotic fear of a school-related object like the bus, a fire alarm, or the lunchroom. Like

any other phobia, while the fear is usually a totally unreasonable one, for the phobic child, it is real and terrifying. The phobic fear is beyond the voluntary control of the child and leads to a complete avoidance of the feared object or situation. While this type of school stress is less common than most, it is devastating for the child and parent who endure it.

Depression and Anxiety

This category of severe school stressors is also a very troublesome one for parents, educators, and mental health professionals. When a child suffers from depression or anxiety, there is no easily identifiable culprit like a traumatic family event or an educational problem that can be blamed. One cannot even point to a feared object or situation that has precipitated the condition. The stress appears to be deep within the child, and mental-health professionals are increasingly recognizing and diagnosing conditions like depression and anxiety in children as the reasons for school refusal. Older children and adolescents with depression often gradually withdraw from their peer group or drop out of extracurricular activities as a precursor to refusing to attend school.

Middle-School Malingerers

Another group of kids who experience school stress are those heading off to middle or junior high school. They are faced with leaving the self-contained classroom cocoon of elementary school and surviving in the junior high jungle with its crowded hallways, gang showers, and breakneck schedules. Middle-school students are more sophisticated about their school refusal behaviors than they were in kindergarten. They don't cling to their mother's legs on the school steps, but they do have headaches and stomachaches. They miss the bus too often and are frequently seen in the nurse's office just about the time gym or math class rolls around. A middle-school student experiencing school stress may be more difficult to identify if he or she never experienced it when younger. Nevertheless, the symptoms are unmistakable—complaints of feeling ill, observable anxiety, and a compelling desire to remain at home.

The Terrible Truants

The terrible truants are a slightly different group of kids who don't go to school. While the truant is chronically absent from school, he doesn't generally hang around home either. In fact, in most cases the truant's parents are unaware that he or she isn't in school. The truant enjoys hanging around strip malls, street corners, shopping centers, movie theaters, or video arcades. The truant is often impulsive and somewhat defiant, exhibiting none of the anxiety, distress, and physical symptoms seen in most children with school stress. The truant is sometimes described as antisocial or delinquent and gives little or no evidence of academic achievement or interests. The truant is on his or her way to a long-term career of finding ways to avoid both school and work.

I'm Here But I Hate Every Minute of It

This category of school stress behavior is one that is rarely recognized or validated in the research literature, but as a principal I heard about it almost daily. This child is one who comes to school every day and does the work, but never stops complaining. The constant whining about problems (whether real or imagined) is maddening. If you listen to it, it can drive you crazy. If you dismiss it, you might not recognize a serious case of school stress.

I'm Here But You Can't Make Me Do the Work

This is another category of school stress behavior that is rarely mentioned in the same breath with the school phobia we defined earlier, but it's a major problem for both parents and educators. This is the child who's at school every day but does nothing. He doesn't do his in-class work and he doesn't do his homework either. This hard-core refuser is blatant in his behavior—uninspired and unintimidated by even the most motivating or terrifying teacher.

High School Dropouts

The final peak of school stress for many young people occurs when they turn sixteen. At this point, when educators and parents can no longer wield the club of compulsory education, many students choose to leave school. Dropping out of high school is the ultimate act of desperation or rebellion for many young people, an

act that all too predictably defines the course of their
future success (or failure) in life.

Any Combination of the Above
Rarely does a case of school stress present a single
identifying symptom that makes for an easy diagnosis.
More often than not, a combination of factors will interact to create the problem.

And Whose Fault Is It?

We are all to blame for school stress—parents, educators, and the larger community. Collectively we must
share the responsibility and together we must work to
solve the problem. All too often, however, we point
fingers at each other. Parents blame principals and
teachers for their kids' school stress. And we educators
are too willing to blame Mom, Dad, or the family tree.

Early Warning Signs

Here are some common early indicators of school
stress. Pay attention to them.

- complaints about fellow students and teachers
- difficulty in getting out of bed; dawdling
- waiting until the last minute to do school-related
  tasks
- a pattern of absences on Mondays and Fridays
- constant negative self-talk about school performance

- disinterest in what is being worn to school and personal grooming
- problems with sleeping; nightmares; regression to bed-wetting
- eating disorders
- calls from the school nurse with nonspecific complaints (for example, headaches or stomachaches with no fever)

To those who are tempted to write off school stress as just a phase kids go through, consider that researchers have tied school phobia to the following problems later in life: high rates of psychiatric disorders[4], multiple phobias[5], work and college avoidance[6], delayed learning[7], suicide[8], academic deterioration, inability to establish meaningful peer relationships, legal conflicts[9], panic attacks, agoraphobia[10], and adult mood disorders[11]. As a principal, I never took the problem lightly. Ignored and left untreated, it can balloon into a major problem that can affect a child's chances for future academic success.

There's a big difference between knowing that your child is experiencing school stress and figuring out what's behind it and how to alleviate it. Chapter 2 provides a checklist to help you isolate the source of your child's distress, and chapter 3 suggests some possible plans of action.

2

What's Behind Your Child's School Stress?

Trying to track down the underlying causes of your child's school stress can create as much consternation and frustration as trying to find a five-year-old income tax return when the IRS calls. In other words, it can make you feel completely helpless. That's why I've put together the School Stress Diagnostic Checklist. Use it to help uncover the specific problems that are creating or contributing to your child's school stress.

School Stress Diagnostic Checklist

Some steps of the checklist are divided into age categories (Early Childhood, four years to third grade; Middle Grades, fourth through sixth grades; and Junior

High/High School, seventh through twelfth grades). Choose the one that matches your child's age. Once you've figured out some possible precipitators to your child's school stress, you'll be ready to implement an intervention from Chapter Three that will get your child happily back in school and keep the problem from recurring in the future.

Step 1: Examine Independence and Confidence Levels

Read through the following descriptions and determine your child's level of independence and self-confidence. A child lacking in independence and self-confidence will be more prone to school stress.

Early Childhood
One of the major causes of school stress in early childhood is separation anxiety. If you answer yes to one or more of the following questions, chances are your child has a full-blown case of it. Take steps to "wean" your child and help her build confidence in her own ability to handle new situations. You might even need some outside support yourself in separating from your child. Often parental feelings of overprotection can transfer a sense of discomfort and insecurity to children and they begin to doubt their own abilities to handle the "real world."

- Has your child always been shy and had a hard time adjusting to new situations?
- Does your child have a history of difficulty in

separating from you? Does your child exhibit chronically clingy behavior, no matter where you try to leave him or her?

- Does your child still want to sleep with you?
- Have you been reluctant to introduce other child-care providers into your home or leave your child in situations like Sunday school because of your child's behavior when you try to leave?

The Middle Grades

We've been relentlessly reminded in recent years about the need for supervising our children. There are so many things to be afraid of—kidnappings, abuse, drugs, and gangs—that letting our children out of our sight, even briefly, makes us nervous. But we need to balance thoughtful supervision with the need to help our children develop confidence and independence. Over-smothered, over-scheduled, and over-supervised kids are prime candidates for school stress. If you answer no to one or more of the following questions, you may be controlling too much of your child's behavior.

- Do you encourage your child to do things on his or her own on the weekends?
- Does your child have some private, personal time for relaxation and play?
- Does your child have opportunities to make choices about what he or she wants to do? wear?
- Are you relaxed when you're not in control of what your child is doing every minute of every day?

Junior High/High School

Letting go of our children really begins when they are toddlers as we gradually give them increasing responsibility and independence and loosen the ties that bind them to us. For some reason, some parents try to reverse this natural process when their children are older, with disastrous results. They give their toddlers total freedom and then gradually begin to tighten control until they have their high schoolers bound and gagged. Remember that when your child enters the junior high and high school years, he or she needs more responsibility, not less.

Step 2: Assess Your Child's Social Skills

If your child is socially immature, he or she is at high risk for school stress. When I was a new teacher, I thought kids came to school to learn. Silly me. They come to be with their friends. If your child doesn't have any friends at school, the motivation to go to school will be reduced and may even disappear. Typical problems that might arise when your child has a social-skills deficit include: fighting; being teased or bullied; inability to cope with school; being ignored; being shy or withdrawn. I've dealt with social skills in more detail in the book, *"Nobody Likes Me": What to Do When Your Child Doesn't Have Friends.* (For more information, see the list of my titles at the end of this book.)

You will need to enlist the help of your child's teacher(s) in determining how socially mature your child is. Answering no to one or more of the questions below probably means your child is socially immature:

- Does my child participate in group activities and class discussions?
- Is my child included in play activities at recess?
- Does my child exhibit socially appropriate behavior?
- Does my child have any friends in the neighborhood or at school?

Step 3: Evaluate Your Child's Academic Skills

If your child has academic problems and his or her academic needs are not being met appropriately, school will be very stressful. If you suspect serious academic problems but don't have a clear understanding of just where your child falls on the achievement continuum, take steps to get a complete academic assessment. Obtain answers to the following questions to help determine your child's academic skills.

- Can your child read, write, and do mathematics at the appropriate grade level for his or her age?
- Does your child have any diagnosed learning disabilities?
- Is there a substantial gap between your child's abilities and his or her achievement?

If you cannot obtain the help you need at school to

assess your child, consult a learning consultant or tutoring center.

Step 4: Consider Personality and Temperament

Drs. Stella Chess, Alexander Thomas, and Herbert Birch conducted the original research on temperament and its effect on personality. They identified nine different aspects of temperament that affect how a child will react to life as it unfolds.[1] Consider where your child falls on the continuum for each of these important qualities:

Activity Level: Is your child 1) very quiet and passive, 2) a whirling dervish constantly in motion, or 3) somewhere in between?

Regularity: Is your child 1) predictable and easy to schedule, 2) sporadic and hard to routinize, or 3) somewhere in between?

Approach/Withdrawal: Is your child 1) outgoing and open to new experiences, 2) slow to enjoy new experiences, clothes, or foods, or 3) somewhere in between?

Adaptability: Is your child 1) adaptable to change, 2) slow to "warm up" in new situations, or 3) somewhere in between?

Sensory Threshold: Is your child 1) oblivious to things like strange odors, temperature, pain, or noises, 2) touchy and conscious of every little irritant in life, or 3) somewhere in between?

Positive/Negative: Is your child almost always 1) happy and easygoing, 2) constantly upset about life's ups and downs, or 3) somewhere in between?

Intensity of Reaction: Are your child's emotional responses 1) easy to read, 2) tough to figure out, or 3) somewhere in between?

Distractibility: Is your child 1) able to concentrate and focus for age-appropriate lengths of time, 2) unable to focus and concentrate at all, or 3) somewhere in between?

Persistence: Is your child 1) willing to stick with a task until it's done, 2) easily frustrated by difficulty, or 3) somewhere in between?

If your child is slow to adapt to new situations, is touchy and conscious of every little irritant, and is easily frustrated by difficulty, his personality and temperament will definitely predispose him to higher levels of school stress. He will need more time to adjust to new situations and will require lots of information and emotional support to deal with any changes in life, even if they are minor.

Step 5: Ask the Right Questions

Begin early to develop rapport and trust with your child. Asking certain questions and responding appropriately to your child's answers will help develop these traits as well as help you determine what may be contributing to school stress. Listed below are some possible questions and areas of concern to pursue in each age category.

Early Childhood
Young children under school stress can sometimes be worried about what's happening at home or conversely be very concerned about some real or imagined aspect of classroom life. They need information and reassurance regarding both places.

- Are you worried about what I'll be doing at home while you're at school?
- Are you worried that I'll start to love the baby more while you're at school?
- Are you afraid I won't come back to pick you up?
- Are you afraid of wetting yourself?
- Are you afraid you won't be able to find the bus after school?
- Are you afraid of anything else at school?

The Middle Grades
Keep the lines of communication open. Be a good listener. Your child may give you noncommittal answers and be unwilling to share details about her school life,

but keep asking. When your child does begin to open up, validate her fears and feelings. Be empathetic. Don't argue with her or make light of her problem and tell her to ignore it. Listening to our children's heartbreaks is difficult for us as parents. We want to "kiss it and make it better" immediately.

- Did you have a fight with your best friend?
- Did somebody make fun of what you were wearing?
- Did the teacher yell at you?
- Did you get picked last for your team in gym?
- Did the kids laugh at you for making a mistake?
- Did somebody tease you on the playground?
- Did somebody do something to you on the bus or the playground?
- Did you get a bad grade on a test?
- Do you have a big test coming up?
- Did you forget to do your homework?
- Are you worried about getting a bad grade?
- Is there an assignment you don't understand?
- Has somebody threatened to do something bad to you if you tell on them?
- Has a teacher threatened or gotten physical with you or other students in the class (for example, slapping, hitting, pinching, pushing, shoving)?
- Has someone brought a gun or knife to school and shown it to you?

Junior High School/High School

I knew my daughter Emily was worried, but I thought

the reason for her depressed demeanor was a spat with her best friend. The real problem came spilling out around the dinner table. A trusted and admired teacher had taunted and teased her inappropriately in front of her friends. He had crossed the boundaries of good judgment and taste, and in the process he shattered her self-esteem. She never wanted to see him again. We discussed several options, and she agreed that her teacher needed to be confronted about his behavior, but she wasn't ready to do it. She asked if I would be willing to talk to him, so I met with the teacher privately and explained our situation. Fortunately, he was remorseful and apologetic. Our meeting paved the way for one he subsequently had with Emily in which he apologized for his behavior, and the fences were mended. But I'm sure Emily will never forget the remark. The scar remains.

- Did a teacher or student say or do something inappropriate (sexual advances, abuse, harassment, teasing)?
- Are you anxious about an upcoming speech you have to give?
- Did somebody have drugs or a weapon at school?
- Are you close to failing one or more of your classes?

Step 6: Examine Your Interaction Patterns

Often the easiest way to change our children's behavior is to change our own first. Your child's symptoms of school stress could well be in response to the way you are interacting with him or her. Take a moment to evaluate your own interaction patterns and if they aren't the best, change.

- Do you talk about the importance of education with your child? (The messages you send—both spoken and unspoken—about the importance of education are powerful reinforcers for your child to attend and do well in school.)

- Do you affirm your confidence in your child to achieve in school? (In the face of failure and discouragement, parents need to believe in their children.)

- Do you talk with your child about what is happening in his or her life? (This is one of the most important things you can do. Get help from a counselor if the lines of communication have broken down.)

- Do you say no to your child when necessary? (Poor discipline is a major contributing factor to school stress. Take a hard look at this aspect of your parenting.)

- Do you worry about your child a great deal? (If you worry excessively about your child, your anxiety is probably spilling over into your parenting. Get help in finding out where your fears are coming from and how to deal with them.)

- Are you a perfectionist for whom nothing less than the best is acceptable? (This kind of parent-

ing style is definitely a contributing factor to
school stress.)

- Do you feel powerless to make a difference in your
  own life or the life of your child?
- Do you compare siblings, holding up the smarter,
  faster child as an example for the others to as-
  pire to? (This parenting practice is inexcusable.
  Stop comparing your children and start treating
  them as the unique, wonderful creations they
  are.)
- Are you willing to learn something new and
  model being a learner in front of your child?

Step 7: Assess Your Child's Health

There are two ways to deal with stressors in one's life:
fight or flight. When people employ the "fight" mecha-
nism their behavior turns outward, and everyone living with them knows that something is wrong. They
cry frequently, have short tempers, and are hostile and
moody. They are uncooperative, pessimistic, and un-
communicative. Those who deal with stress through
"flight" turn their anxiety inward, resulting in a variety of physical complaints: headaches; stomach problems like diarrhea, constipation, and nausea; muscle
jerks or tics; eating disorders; sleeping disorders; faint-
ing; a general feeling of tiredness; shortness of breath;
teeth grinding; stuttering; dizziness.

There are some genuine physical problems like allergies, infections (sinus, strep, ear), and other chronic
illnesses that are not a result of stress and need to be

treated. Seven-year-old Carson didn't want to get out of bed. Moody and listless, he refused to get dressed for school. Naturally, his mother took him to the doctor where he was pronounced fit as a fiddle. She begged, cajoled, and threatened Carson day after day but couldn't get him off to school. Carson's mom began to think she had a full-blown case of school stress on her hands. Carson continued to mope around the house, so mom took him to another doctor. Again, Carson received a clean bill of health. There were also no apparent sources of school stress that could have caused Carson's listlessness, and he'd always been a top student. So his mother persevered and took him to yet another doctor who diagnosed Carson with a serious sinus infection. After a round of antibiotics, Carson was once again an eager learner. Follow your best parental instincts and have your child thoroughly evaluated by a physician (or physicians) who can rule out any medical problems.

A child with Attention Deficit and Hyperactivity Disorder (ADHD) often exhibits major symptoms of school stress. Being unable to fit in, measure up, or produce in the way that everyone keeps saying he can and should is incredibly stressful. Once a child has been diagnosed, and appropriate medical and educational interventions have been prescribed, the stress should lessen. However, school will almost always be more stressful for kids with ADHD.

Finally, if your child acts depressed or apathetic, or even talks about ending his or her life or harming someone else, take this situation seriously. Don't ignore any of the following warning signals based on statistics from the National Center for Health. If your child exhibits any of these behaviors, seek professional help immediately.

- Preoccupation with themes of death, or expressing suicidal thoughts
- Giving away prized possessions
- Changes in sleeping patterns—too much or too little
- Sudden and extreme changes in eating habits; losing or gaining weight
- Withdrawal from friends and family
- Changes in school performance (lowered grades, cutting classes, dropping out of activities)
- Personality changes such as nervousness, outbursts of anger, or apathy about appearance and health
- Use of drugs or alcohol
- Recent suicide of friend or relative
- Previous suicide attempt

Step 8: Examine Your Family Interaction Patterns

Unhealthy family interaction patterns can contribute to your child's school stress. If one or more of the following inappropriate parenting practices is present in your family, consider counseling to work on your problems.

- Parents who disagree on how the children should be disciplined.

- Parents who are not equally committed to solving the school stress problem.
- Parents who do not spend time together and share activities and interests with the children.
- Family members who fail to respect each other's opinions and feelings.
- One parent who aligns with a child against the other parent.
- A parent who is overly dependent and emotionally involved with a child.

Step 9: Consider Your Own Feelings

If the thought of school causes you stress, you could well be transmitting your anxieties to your child. Maybe you need some assistance in dealing with your own brand of "school stress" before you can help your child.

- Do you constantly criticize the school administration and teachers?
- Did you experience failure in school?
- Did you have bad experiences with teachers when you were in school?
- Do you feel anxious when you have to face a school conference?

Step 10: Measure Your Family's Stress Levels

If your family's stress levels are off the chart because of specific events or because of your frenetic, frenzied lifestyle, start saying no and simplify your life.

- Are you experiencing any of the major life stressors, such as a job change, financial difficulty, an addition to the family, or a move?
- Are you a single parent?
- Are you a dual-career family?
- Do you need multiple calendars to keep track of your family's activities (church, Scouts, sports, music lessons, school events)?
- Do you rarely have time for family meals together because of travel, work, or recreational/extra-curricular schedules?

Step 11: Consider Your Child's Stress Levels

Kids, like adults, are affected by the major life stressors such as a death, moving, or a new baby. One family I know is off the charts in the stress department: two job losses—one firing and one layoff, one major move, one death, one addition to the family, one major construction project, one business start-up, and one change in financial status. Amazingly, the children in this family are not showing signs of school stress, but it wouldn't be surprising if they were.

Step 12: Listen to Those Who Know Your Child.

I know how difficult it is for parents (myself included)

to get bad reviews about the way we parent or the way our children behave. Like the Muppet Miss Piggy, who is always incredulous when confronted with her outrageous behavior, we react to the truth about our children or ourselves with disbelief: "Moi?" Yes, you. I can't tell you how many times I've counseled with parents of kindergarten or first-grade students to alert them to school stress issues only to be met with icy stares and defensive attitudes. I've also had those same parents return years later to bemoan the even bigger problem that faced them because they chose to ignore advice from others who were perhaps wiser and definitely more objective about their child. If a teacher, counselor, neighbor, or friend who knows your child well shares a concern, at least think about it before you reject it outright. Early intervention is the best answer for school stress.

Step 13: Examine the School Environment

The school environment itself could be a major source of your child's school stress. There are several areas of the school environment to examine for potential trouble.

Academic Discrimination
There are many ways your child could be academically discriminated against in school, each of which can be a source of school stress.

- Is your child a low-achiever who is on the receiving end of differential treatment by teachers?

(Low achievers have been shown to be given fewer opportunities to participate, less choice about their work in the classroom, and lower expectations from teachers).

- Is your student tracked into a "low" reading group in elementary school, or bottom-level classes in middle school or high school, with no hope of ever getting out?
- Does your child have access to computers, the school library, and art, music, and physical education activities?

Classroom Conditions

If you have doubts about what is happening in your child's classroom, obtain permission to visit for an hour. Keep your eyes and ears open. If you see any of the following signs of a stressful classroom, you should take steps to alert a school administrator. If the conditions are serious enough, you may need to remove your child from the classroom as soon as possible.

- Are the children in the class bored, inattentive, unruly, or too tightly controlled?
- Are consequences for bad behavior too harsh and punitive?
- Is the room messy, cluttered, or disorganized?
- Is the teacher confused, unfocused, disorganized, or uninteresting?
- Are learning materials outdated or in short supply?

- Are children unable to talk or move about at appropriate intervals?
- Is there a clear distinction in the class between the "haves" and the "have-nots" (for example, do the low-achievers sit on one side of the classroom and the high-achievers on the other)?

Teacher Effectiveness

Spending a thousand hours in one year with incompetent or ineffective teachers can be a major cause of school stress for any child. Do whatever you can to make sure your child has the best teachers.

- Are the teachers confident that all children can learn?
- Are the teachers enthusiastic about teaching the basic subjects?
- Do teachers know and support the educational philosophy, academic policies, and priorities of the school?
- Are teachers good models of conduct and academic commitment?
- Are teachers well-educated in general and in the subjects they teach?
- Are teachers available to students for special help on academic or personal problems?
- Are teachers well-prepared for class? Do they start and end class promptly? Do they use class time for teaching and learning?
- Do teachers speak and write well?

- Are teachers cooperative and supportive of each other and the administration?

School Climate

Your child must feel safe and secure in school to be free of school stress. Evaluate the following aspects of your child's school climate to determine if safety and security (physical, emotional, and psychological) are a problem.

- Has the school published a statement of expectations and standards for the conduct of staff and students?
- Are such statements widely understood and accepted?
- Does the school have a strong sense of community?
- Does the school cooperate with parents and civic agencies on disciplinary matters?
- Do students have positions of responsibility for student activities, conduct, and school property?
- Do students and staff members have numerous opportunities to work jointly on school projects?
- Do staff members have consistent disciplinary values and practices throughout the school, as opposed to having different standards in each classroom?
- Are students praised for good performance?
- Do students believe that staff members genuinely care about their well-being?

- Is the tone of the staff businesslike and professional yet interested in the students?
- Do staff members spot problems early and respond quickly and firmly?
- Are reprimands delivered quietly, without disrupting class?
- Are parents notified of discipline problems with their children?
- Does the school keep useful records of delinquency, truancy, disruption, vandalism, tardiness, absences, and other kinds of anti-school behavior?
- Is the school clean and well-maintained? Are needed repairs made promptly?

I hope that you have been able to identify which of the variables in this chapter (from a lack of self-confidence and independence to an unhealthy or unsafe school environment) may be affecting your child's chances for a stress-free school year. Chapters 3 and 4 contain suggestions for how to alleviate school stress and get your child back into school and learning.

3

Getting Them Back to School

Whenever school stress rears its ugly head at your house, don't think "this too shall pass," and then wait for a "miracle." Research shows a strong relationship between the *speed* with which an intervention to end school stress was started and the remission of the acute symptoms. The longer you wait to solve a school-stress problem, the greater the possibility of its becoming chronic and long-standing.

One of the most valued members of my staff when I was an elementary school principal was my health aide. After the morning bell she collected attendance folders from each teacher and compared the list of absentees with the messages on her voice-mail system from parents reporting their children absent. Often, a bit of clever detective work on the part of the aide uncovered a full-blown case of school stress. The complaints phoned in were usually nonspecific (headache, stomachache, not feeling well). But the more revealing aspect was the unmistakable patterns—lots of Monday and Friday absences with several longer stretches of absence here and there. "I think we've got a problem here," my aide would announce in solemn tones. "It's time to bring out the big gun." That meant she wanted me to call and find out just what was going on.

Invariably I would discover a student who was finding it increasingly difficult to get out of bed and face the classroom. That's when I would recommend an immediate intervention to get the child back in school. With each passing day out of school, students lose ground—academically, socially, and emotionally. The old proverb about getting back on the horse immediately after you fall off has some application in these instances. The longer a child enjoys the attention of parents, the security of his or her own home, and the freedom to watch television, eat ice cream, and play video games, the harder the struggle for the parent and the greater the trauma of returning to the classroom for the student.

If your child is younger, and extreme school stress has happened recently and seemingly out-of-the-blue, implement Plan One that follows. If your child is a chronic school refuser or older in age, implement Plan Two. Implement Plan Three if your child is seriously truant from school and at risk of becoming a dropout.

During and after the implementation of these plans, begin to make the changes in your home life that will 1) help you as a parent to assist your child to deal more effectively with his or her personal anxieties; 2) establish positive patterns among the family as a whole that will help alleviate school stress; and 3) foster a team approach to solving the school stress problem.

In order for any of the plans to work, everyone involved must overcome any anxieties about helping the child. It's natural to identify the child as the anxious player in the drama, but I've seen more than my share of adults who melt like marshmallows when confronted with a child who "won't go." Teachers become defensive about their role; courageous administrators who think nothing of facing the school board fall apart; and parents are suddenly spineless. All the participants must send the same message to the child: "We know you're afraid, and we're here to help you. We care about you. We believe in you. You are able to go to school, and you're going to go to school. We will not be moved by tears or tantrums. You will survive. And . . . you *will* go to school." Everyone must remain adamant about the need for the child to continue attending school.

Plan One

1. Enjoy a pleasant and relaxing weekend with your child. Don't talk about school attendance until Sunday evening. Before bedtime, tell the child that he or she will be attending school on Monday morning. Be firm, calm, and very pleasant. Do not argue or discuss the decision with the child.

2. Take the child to school on Monday morning. If neither parent is able to take the child to school, arrange with school personnel to pick up the child. (Be sure to execute a signed permission note allowing school personnel to transport your child.) Some children will be more willing to come out of their house or apartment on their own if someone from school is waiting to pick them up.

3. Arrange in advance for someone to meet the child at the school door. (It's not a good idea for this person to be the teacher since he or she has multiple tasks and responsibilities before school. The principal or counselor is recommended.)

4. Leave immediately after turning your child over to school personnel. Do not go into the school building, look back, or call the office to see how things are going. Don't walk around the building and look in the classroom window. Just leave! You will undermine the whole plan if your resolve is not firm on this issue.

5. On Monday evening, tell your child how pleased you are that she went to school. Even if she had a terrible time and was very upset for most of the morning, tell her how pleased you are. Even if by afternoon she "developed a fever" and had to be picked up at the nurse's office, praise her. And tell her that Tuesday will be much better.

6. On Tuesday, take your child to school once again where she will be met by school personnel and escorted to her classroom.

7. Continue with the plan throughout the week. On the evening of the first symptom-free day, have a party to celebrate your child's achievements. Most children have a symptom-free day near the end of the first week. Stubborn, strong-willed school refusers may need another week to reach the goal. Do not give up. Be firm.

Plan Two

Plan Two is designed for hard-core, long-term school refusers. If you are living with a child or young person in this category, you have no doubt tried many different plans. Or you've tried something for a day or two and then you've slipped back to square one. Here are the steps to follow:

1. Ask the school to put together an intervention team made up of the child's teacher(s), school nurse, school psychologist, school social worker, any outside professionals who may be working with the child (tutor, counselor, psychologist, physician), your spouse, and you.

2. Hold a team meeting to share information about the child's academic, social, and emotional needs. All participants in this meeting must agree to

work together in the child's best interests. Unfortunately, the team members often want to point fingers at each other. Parents want to blame school personnel for their child's strong distaste for school. School personnel believe that if the parents were doing their job, the child would be in school. And the child meanwhile is falling between the cracks. All parties must work together for the good of the child. Here's the agenda for the team to accomplish:

☐ Select a case manager/chairperson and secretary. The case manager/chairperson will monitor the effectiveness of the intervention, and the secretary will keep careful records of all aspects of it.

☐ Determine daily expectations for the child (for example, he will attend half a day for two days, then full days after that).

☐ Determine who will be responsible for getting the child to school (bus, parent, school personnel). Make sure you sign a permission note for school personnel to transport your child.

☐ Determine a backup plan if a panic reaction occurs.

☐ Determine if any modifications in the academic schedule or a change of teachers or teacher expectations will be made.

☐ Determine what the response of the teacher should be if the student has physical complaints, as well as the response of the nurse if the student comes to the health office. If the student is a "runner" (that is, might run away from school if given the opportunity), determine how the school will supervise the child to ensure this won't happen.

☐ Determine if the school will provide counseling services.

☐ Agree on a consistent manner in which the student will be confronted when he or she asks to go home.

☐ Agree on a contingency plan if any of the key team members are absent on Monday.

3. Enjoy a pleasant and relaxing weekend with your child. Don't talk about school attendance until Sunday evening. Before bedtime, tell the child that he or she will be attending school on Monday morning. Be firm, calm, and very pleasant. Do not argue or discuss the decision with the child.

4. Take the child to school on Monday morning (or

arrange for transportation). Make sure the transportation arrangements are well planned and tightly controlled.

5. Arrange in advance for someone to meet the child at the school door. (This person should be someone other than the teacher since he or she has multiple tasks and responsibilities before school. The principal or counselor is recommended.)

6. Leave immediately after turning your child over to school personnel. Do not go into the school building, look back, or call the office. Don't walk around the building and look in the classroom window. Just leave!

7. On Monday evening, tell your child how pleased you are that he went to school. Even if he had a terrible time and was very upset for most of the morning, tell him how pleased you are. Even if by afternoon he "developed a stomachache" and had to be picked up at the nurse's office, praise him. And tell him that Tuesday will be much better.

8. On Tuesday, take your child to school once again where he will be met by school personnel and escorted to his classroom.

9. Continue with the plan throughout the week. On the evening of the first symptom-free day, have a party to celebrate your child's achievements.

This plan is a very basic and straightforward approach to the problem. Team members who know and have worked with your child may choose to include some variations that meet the specific needs of your child. As with any plan, common sense is needed. Keep these principles in mind:

- Keep the plan as simple as possible. When a plan is too complicated for the staff or parents to follow, it won't work.
- Make sure everyone has the resources they need to follow through on the plan (time and extra staff members to escort or transport the child; time and extra staff members to provide supervision for time-outs or counseling).
- Make sure the key staff members who will implement the plan have had a chance to help design it. When people aren't involved in the planning, they have a tendency to become critical and uncooperative.

Plan Three

Dealing with elementary school truants is fairly simple. Plan Two will usually work. Incentives, parent/student contracts, or loss of privileges will usually remediate a younger truant, particularly if these interventions are coupled with counseling and academic assistance. When a child is older and the reasons for his truancy are undoubtedly long-standing and complex, then the consequences frequently prescribed for truancy, such as in-school suspension, expulsion, and after-school detention, work on a very limited scale. Creativity, resourcefulness, and flexibility are the keys to getting your older, stronger, truant child back in school. Here's the plan.

1. Ask the school to put together an intervention team made up of the child's teacher(s), school nurse, school psychologist, school social worker, and any outside professionals who may be working with the child (tutor, counselor, psychologist, physician). Of course, you and your spouse will be an integral part of the team.

2. Hold a team meeting to share information about the child's academic, social, and emotional needs. All participants in this meeting must agree to work together in the child's best interests. Unfortunately, the team members often want to point fingers at each other. Parents want to blame school personnel for their child's strong distaste in and distrust of school. School personnel believe that if the parents were doing their job, the child would be in school. And the child, meanwhile, is falling between the cracks. All parties must work together for the good of the child.

3. Here's the agenda for the team to accomplish:

   ☐ Select a case manager/chairperson and secretary. The case manager/chairperson will monitor the effectiveness of the intervention, and the secretary will keep careful records of all aspects of it.

☐ Evaluate the possible sources of school stress for the truant child (for example, family, school, personal).

☐ Review what interventions or plans have been tried in the past and what aspects of them have been successful and unsuccessful.

☐ Assign a team member to conduct an in-depth interview with the student. The purpose of this interview will be to determine what aspects of school life he or she would like to see changed to make attendance a more attractive option.

☐ Determine what new interventions might work, keeping in mind the student's input. Be creative. Listed below are some possibilities that have worked in other school settings. But when you put together a team of professionals who care about a child, their ability to come up with a creative plan will surpass anything I've suggested here.

a) Require the student to telephone school at 7:00 each morning. If the call is not received, a teacher, administrator, or other staff member will call the student.

b) Assign a community mentor to the student who will encourage him or her and help to monitor school attendance.

c) Arrange for attendance at an alternative or vocational school.

d) Assign a student buddy to the truant (providing wake-up calls to each other, holding each other accountable to complete assignments).

e) Offer to make a daily wake-up call if the student is habitually late. (I have even purchased alarm clocks for students who needed an extra incentive.)

f) Offer a homework hotline for academic assistance.

g) Ease the re-entry to school by shortening the school day by prearrangement so the student will at least attend half of his or her classes in the beginning.

h) Schedule a conference with the student and determine which aspects of school are most responsible for his or her truancy (teacher wasting the student's time; classes irrelevant to the student; difficulty with coursework; failing tests; etc.). Remediate those problems by changing teachers or class assignments or providing a tutor.

i) Offer special field trips for perfect attendance.

j) Assign a peer tutor from each of the truant's classes who can be called for homework help.

k) Arrange a work-study program in which a student will receive credit for work in the community.

l) Arrange for a supportive family in the neighborhood or church to take the child for a short period to separate the parents and student.

m) Reassign the student to teachers who are more supportive and helpful.

n) Assign a faculty mentor who will meet with the student once weekly to talk about problems.

4. Once the plan has been developed, assign responsibilities to team members, and meet with the student to discuss all aspects of the plan. If possible, the student should attend at least one team meeting to participate in the final drafting of the plan.

5. Obtain the student's signature on a contract agreeing to meet the terms of the plan for a specified period of time. At the end of this time period, the plan will be evaluated and fine-tuned. Keep the following principles in mind as the plan is developed:

- Keep the plan as simple as possible. When a plan is too complicated for the staff or parents to follow, it won't work.
- Make sure everyone has the resources they need to follow through on the plan (time and extra staff members to escort or transport the child; time and extra staff members to provide counseling).
- Make sure the key staff members who will implement the plan have had a chance to help design it. When people aren't involved in the planning, they have a tendency to become critical and uncooperative.

Plan Three is not foolproof. There are some young people who are dead set on their drop-out plans. Remain calm in the face of this devastating news and make the best of it. One family found that their son's talents were not being tapped in the regular academic program. He has enrolled in a vocational program and is training to become an auto mechanic. One family decided that their daughter's severe learning disability made functioning in the regular classroom almost impossible for her. They hired a private tutor to prepare her for the high school equivalency exam, and she is working part-time in a beauty shop. In one case in which a young man decided to drop out of school, his parents developed a contract for him. He agreed to get a full-time job, pay rent, and follow the rules of the house. By the end of the year he had decided to re-enter high school and work for his diploma. His experiences in the real world convinced him of the value of education. He's on the honor roll now. His parents remained calm, supportive, but firm through the ordeal.

Implementing any of these plans is only the beginning to solving the school stress problem at your house. Now that you have your child physically back in school, you will need to take some other steps to eliminate or reduce the stress that caused him or her to want to stay home in the first place. Chapter 4 contains a wide variety of ideas and activities to help reduce school stress.

4

Fifty Fabulous
Ways to Reduce
School Stress

Once you have used one of the intervention plans described in chapter 3 to get your child back in school, there are many things you can be doing to reduce school stress. Some of the activities that follow are simple to incorporate into your family life; others are more complex and time-consuming. Read through the entire list before you decide which ones you wish to try. It's better to choose just one activity and experience success than to bite off more than you can chew.

1. Share the Burden
Share your problem with a trusted counselor, friend, or educator. Step back and solicit an objective viewpoint from someone who knows you and your family. Perhaps you are too involved to see where the problem

really lies. Gain perspective from someone who has successfully parented grown children. Cry on someone's shoulder, and the problem will seem less stressful.

2. Academic Testing

Whenever a child is experiencing severe school stress, I recommend comprehensive academic testing to gather further information about that child's learning abilities. If your child is not eligible for testing at school, find an independent learning specialist. Although the process could be costly, the expenditure will be worth every penny. Don't subscribe to the old line that "he's just not applying himself," or "if she'd settle down and get to work, she'd make better grades." Imagine how stressful life can be for a child if she has an undiagnosed attention or learning disorder. Determine if your child has one.

3. Stick Out Your Tongue and Say "Ah"

Have your child examined by a physician to rule out the possibility that a medical problem could be at the root of his or her school stress. Allergies and chronic infections can make kids irritable, depressed, uncooperative, and inattentive. Also, certain medications have been successfully used in the treatment of school phobia when anxiety and depression are involved. Once a child is less depressed and anxious, a forced return to school with counseling will be more effective.

4. Tell Me All about It

If your budget permits, schedule an appointment for

your child to see a psychologist or counselor who specializes in working with children. Sometimes a skilled therapist can uncover the issue behind the school phobia and help your child (and/or your family) develop more effective coping skills.

5. The Stress-Free Classroom

Check out the stress levels in your child's classroom. Does his teacher like him? Does she treat him with dignity and respect? Does she believe that he can learn? Does she believe that everyone in the class can learn? When you visit or volunteer in the classroom, is there a relaxed, but business-like atmosphere? Or do you feel tense, irritable, and angry? Be an advocate for your child. If you are unhappy with what you find, consult chapter 5 for recommendations about changing classrooms or schools or read *Solving School Problems: Kindergarten through Middle School*.

6. The Safe and Orderly School

Find out all that you can about the school your child attends. Talk to staff members such as bus drivers, custodians, secretaries, and lunch room supervisors. They will have a different perspective about discipline, consistency, and structure than the teachers and principal, and you may be surprised at their observations. Check out the cleanliness and maintenance of the school. Do students and staff take pride in their building? If you find that your child's school is neither safe nor orderly, you have two choices—push for change or withdraw your child.

7. Nobody Likes Me

Kids go to school to be with their friends, and if your child doesn't have any friends, school will be filled with stress. Begin to teach your child some simple friendship behaviors and manners that will help her make friends at school. Among other resources, my book *"Nobody Likes Me": What to Do When Your Child Doesn't Have Friends* contains dozens of practical and easy activities that any parent can put into practice to help his or her child make friends.

8. Building a Caring Community

Ask your child's teacher if he or she would be willing to teach a social skills unit to the entire class. Many schools use the cooperative learning technique in which children work in small heterogeneous groups to accomplish assignments and projects. In order for children to be successful at cooperative learning, they must have well-developed social skills. When kids learn how to work together and help each other, everybody's happier, and the kids learn more.

9. A Circle of Friends

If the curriculum is too crowded for the classroom teacher to take on the task of teaching social skills, ask if the school psychologist or social worker would be able to conduct a small social-skills group made up of students from your child's class.

10. Building Confidence and Independence

The greater your child's confidence and independence,

the less likely that he or she will encounter the worry,
fear, and anxiety that are always a part of school
stress. The confident and independent child can sail
through even the toughest waters without capsizing.
How can you encourage and nurture these two important qualities? Read chapter 6, which contains dozens
of simple things you can do with your child to develop
confidence and independence.

11. Keep It Simple
Simplify and streamline your home life. Start saying
no and building in more time for family fun and one-
on-one child/parent time.

12. 1-2-3 Magic
Sign up for a parenting class to help you get a better
grip on discipline or communication at your house.
Take the class with your spouse so you're both on the
same page. Many parents I know have benefitted
from using Thomas Phelan's excellent video and
book *1-2-3 Magic* as a basis for a discussion group.[1]
Dorothy Rich's *Megaskills* program is also recommended for networking with other parents to learn
about ways to help children become confident and ca-
pable learners.[2]

13. Get Involved
Get involved at your child's school. Getting to know
staff members and administrators on a more personal
level will reduce your own anxiety about schools and
teachers. Find a way to feel at home.

14. Learning Together

Sign up for a parent/child class and be a learner with
your child. Whether you learn to swim, knit, or play
soccer, doing it together will build memories as well as
a meaningful relationship. Be prepared for your child
to be more skilled than you are. I took a computer class
with my son and he left me in the dust.

15. Say Good-bye

Sometimes you have to face the reality that a bad
situation will never improve. That's the time to withdraw and choose another schooling option. Remember
that your child's academic success for a lifetime may
be at stake. See chapter 5 for further suggestions.

16. Home Sweet Home

I don't recommend the homeschooling option for students who are refusing to attend school or have serious
panic and anxiety issues. Their problems may only be
exacerbated in a home-school setting. At the very least,
this option means that the problem is delayed, not
solved. But for situations where the current school or
teacher are unacceptable alternatives, consider homeschooling your child. The Malones did it for just one
semester; it was the perfect answer to an untenable
situation. Their fifth-grade son, Kevin, was a straight
A, happy-go-lucky student until he ended up in Mrs.
Warner's class. She was distant and harsh, unlike any
teacher he'd encountered in his school career. The
harder he worked, the lower his grades seemed to go.
The school's policy made it impossible for the Malones

to get a transfer to another teacher. They opted for a single semester of homeschooling, and Kevin was then off to middle school with nary a problem.

17. Private School
Often (although not always) a private school will offer a more intimate and caring school environment. This may be just what your child needs to recover from a traumatic experience elsewhere. Of course, if your child's school stress started in a private school, consider trying the public school as an alternative. Sometimes if your child has special learning needs, the public school will have more resources.

18. Family Counseling
If your family is floundering because of some situations that have caused serious stress (divorce, separation, unemployment, abuse, death, or any of the other events listed in chapter 2), seek counseling to help you deal with your problems. Local churches and social service agencies frequently offer counseling on an affordable sliding scale.

19. The Princess/Prince and the Pea
Don't fight the fact that your child is hyper-sensitive or slow to warm up to new situations. Prepare her for new experiences ahead of time by role-playing or rehearsing. Your child will gain confidence from some advance warning, and being able to think ahead about what to say and how to act will make her less prone to worrying, temper tantrums, crying jags, and stubborn refusal.

20. Care to Get the Very Best

How are students assigned to teachers in your school? Do the previous year's teachers make the decision about which kids go where, or does the principal have all the power? Are the decisions based on academic standing (Mrs. Jones gets all the "high" kids and Mrs. Smith gets all the "low" kids)? The system works a little differently in each school, so do your homework. Do everything possible (within the boundaries of school policy and good judgment) to obtain the best teacher for your child. Plug into the informal communication network in your neighborhood and you'll soon know how the game is played.

21. The Buzzards vs. the Bluebirds

Being in the lower "Buzzards" reading group in first grade is the first step to big-time school stress. As an elementary-school principal, I worked with my staff to eliminate "fixed-in-stone" ability groups in reading and designed lessons around learning techniques that gave every child an equal chance to learn. Work to eliminate academic discrimination against your child.

22. Coping Techniques

Structure activities to help your child cope with his or her fears and anxieties. For example, teach test-taking strategies to eliminate test anxiety. Or practice dealing with teasing on the playground through role-playing. If you don't feel comfortable helping your child yourself, find a tutor, mentor, or relative to help.

23. Florence Nightingale to the Rescue

Enlist the help of the health aide or school nurse in your school. He or she will be the first person to interact with your child when he complains of a headache or stomachache. When a child is likely feigning sickness, an empathetic school nurse can be a good listener and encourager. A few minutes of TLC might be all that is needed to speed a young learner back to class. Sometimes a child will share concerns about a teacher or other situation in the privacy of the health office that he or she will not talk about anywhere else. Of course, if your child repeatedly complains of aches and pains, see your family physician to rule out a real medical problem.

24. Go to the Top

Enlist the help of the principal in solving your school stress problem. Principals don't control everything in a school, but the good ones are wise, understanding, and have seen hundreds of kids pass through their hallways. Their advice is worth listening to. Principals are usually in charge of placing students in classrooms and can help you avoid an over-controlling teacher or one who takes all student problems and misbehavior as a personal affront. The principal is in charge of safety concerns, the discipline policy, hiring the best possible teachers, and finding ways to remediate the not-so-good ones. Your school principal should make you feel that you and your child are important and that he or she will do everything reasonably possible to solve your problem.

25. An Apple for the Teacher

The cooperation and support of your child's teacher are essential to solving the school stress problem. Here are some things caring teachers do for students who are experiencing school stress, and, in particular, for students who are having difficulty separating from their parents for the first time:

- Allow the child to bring a favorite object from home to school.
- Work out a plan of one phone call home per day.
- Appoint a classroom buddy to help the child.
- Have a classroom discussion about fears.

Here are some other things teachers might do to help a child under severe school stress:

- Be kind but firm with the child. Too much sympathy can backfire.
- Give the child brief timeouts if the child's crying is disturbing the rest of the class.
- Continually assure the child that the next day will be better.
- Offer plenty of verbal reinforcement and praise to the child.
- Smile at the child frequently.
- Stand or sit near the child and offer comforting pats on the back. (Some children react negatively to touch. The teacher needs to be sensitive to this possibility.)

- Give special classroom responsibilities to the child to increase his or her confidence and comfort level.
- If the student feels panicky in the classroom, allow him or her to sit in a seat by the door.
- Avoid calling attention to the child, and avoid calling on the child for discussion or response for a week or two after his or her return from a long absence.

26. Unsung Heroes
School counselors are rarely seen by the average parent, but they can sometimes work wonders for troubled students. The counselor's office is a safe place for a child to identify and express fears or thoughts that automatically are associated with anxious feelings. The counselor can also reinforce and encourage your child's skills in coping with feared situations.

27. Child Advocate
Identify a special advocate or friend for your child at school (for example, the principal, health aide, art teacher, PE teacher, or even a favorite teacher from an earlier grade). This individual would seek out your child during the school day—just to talk, to ask how things are going, or to tell your child that he or she was missed when absent. In addition, this person would make it a point to speak positively in defense of your child to other faculty members if the advocate heard criticism of your child in the faculty lounge (this is unprofessional, but it still happens).

28. Listen Up

One of the most important things you can do for your child is to listen to her concerns and validate her feelings. You don't need to solve a problem on the spot. Sometimes giving "wordless advice" (for example, letting the child talk out the solution on his or her own while you say nothing) is the best thing you can do. Give your child permission to have feelings of fear and uncertainty. Accompany your listening with a close physical presence and a hug.

29. Honesty Is the Best Policy

Be honest with your child about what is happening in your life, but don't use your child as a confidante. Find someone your own age with whom to talk over your personal problems. It's not healthy to have a friendship-based relationship with your child. (Single parents often fall into this trap.) Your child needs a parent, not a peer.

30. Ask My Opinion

Consult with your child regarding any possible change in placement (change of school, change of teacher) you might be considering or your plan could backfire on you.

31. Playground Bullies

Playground bullying should not be shrugged off or lightly dismissed. It's serious and a major source of school stress for children. Do not permit your child to be bullied. Take steps to find out what is really happening (don't assume your child is necessarily telling you the complete story), and then enlist the help of the principal and teachers to deal with the problem. If they refuse to take the matter seriously, take your concerns to the superintendent and the board of education.

32. Role Models

Do you have an attention or learning problem of your own that is causing stress in your life? Learning to manage your *own* disorders will make you better able to help your child cope. There are many resources for this, including my book *Managing Attention and Learning Disorders: A Handbook for Adults*. (For more information, see listing at the end of this book.)

33. Read to Me

The most valuable activity you can share with your child is to read aloud. You must do it every day. No excuses are acceptable. No questions, quizzes, or lessons need accompany the story. Just quietly read together. Read a story about school stress and fears; read a story about courage and bravery; read a funny story that makes you both laugh. I believe that if every parent in this nation read aloud to their children for twenty minutes every night, starting when they were six months old and continuing until they were seven or eight years old, there would be far fewer juvenile delinquents, far fewer at-risk kids, and far fewer kids with school stress. Actually, there would be fewer parents with stress, too. If you're not doing it, start today.

34. Keep in Touch

If you've recently moved and your child misses former
friends and classmates, schedule a weekly telephone
call or, if possible, periodic visits to the old neighborhood. When new friends are made, the phone calls and
visits will be less important. But they will help to
make the transition less stressful.

35. Early Warning System

Children who are most susceptible to school stress are
usually not flexible or easygoing. They need plenty of
advance warning about new projects or changes in the
schedule. Learn to plan ahead, and take time to give
your child the information and practice he or she
needs to cope with change.

36. Have a Teacher for Tea

Invite your child's teacher to your home and get to
know him or her as an individual. In our family, we
invited our children's teachers for lunch each spring.
As the children got older, we kept adding the previous
years' teachers and soon had to hold a Christmas cof-
fee to accommodate the crowd.

37. Dining In

The second-most-important thing to do as family (after
reading aloud) is to eat dinner together and talk. Eat
at least three family dinners together per week. Have
you forgotten what it's like to gather around the dinner table and share stories and experiences? Zapping
your dinner in the microwave and carrying it to the TV

or to your bedroom has too frequently become the norm in many families. Eating dinner together can help keep little problems from becoming big ones.

38. Family Fun

Now I'm going to get radical and suggest that you schedule at least one family outing or activity together per month. It doesn't have to be expensive or time-consuming. Just do something with the whole family together . . . rake leaves, go to the zoo, pick out the Christmas tree, or just sit together in church. It's hard to believe that some kids and adults are even part of the same family because they're never seen at the same time in the same place, not even at home. This will help take care of any problems that weren't solved by reading aloud and eating three meals together per week.

39. Bedtime Chats and Prayers

I've suggested bedtime chats in other books I've written on other topics, but bedtime chats are especially helpful if your child is experiencing school stress. Connecting with your child prior to bedtime in the intimacy of the bedroom can soothe, calm, and heal a troubled spirit. Follow the chat with bedtime prayers as a wonderful way to end the day. Leave your child's cares and worries with God. The assurance that God loves her and will help to solve her school problems is powerful. My husband and I have bedtime chats every night. After we talk, we read a portion of the Bible and pray for our friends and family. Problems that seemed insurmountable will become more manageable after bedtime chats and prayers.

40. See Your Child as He/She Will Become

It's hard for me to believe that the confident world traveler that my twenty-something daughter has become was once a fearful and hesitant kindergartner. She has lived and worked on two continents (in addition to North America), speaks Gaelic and Japanese, and is working on her doctorate in anthropology. I also have to remind myself that my son, who drove his fourth-grade teacher to distraction with his constant need for reassurance, has lived and worked in several Latin American countries and speaks Spanish fluently. It's hard to see our children as they will become and not as they are. We need to believe in them, support them, and encourage them, especially when they are experiencing school stress.

41. Your Child's Learning Style

Determine your child's preferred learning style. Understanding your child's strengths will help you when you want to teach your child something at home, but this knowledge also enables you to be a more effective advocate for your child in school. A book I have found especially helpful in this area is *In Their Own Way: Discovering and Encouraging Your Child's Personal Learning Style.*[3]

42. Hire a Tutor

Consider hiring a learning coach or tutor. Make sure

you get a warm and caring individual who also has top-notch teaching skills. Your child may thrive in a one-to-one atmosphere and be able to make remarkable progress that in turn will give him or her more confidence.

43. Bite Your Tongue
Stop being critical—of yourself, your child, his or her siblings, your spouse, your neighbors, the school, etc. If there's a problem with someone, address it directly but in a caring and compassionate way with that individual. Your constant criticism and harping could well be one source of your child's stress.

44. The Tricks of the Trade
There are dozens of strategies—test-taking, reading comprehension, organizational—that can help your child be a more successful student. (See, for example, my book, *"The Dog Ate It": Conquering Homework Hassles.*)

45. Sweet Dreams
Make sure your children's sleeping schedules are as regular as possible. Children who are fatigued are at risk for school stress. Stick to a regular bedtime and use the pre-bedtime hour for chats, reading, and prayers to ease your children into sound, healthful sleep.

46. For the Sake of the Children
Try to work cooperatively and collaboratively with your ex-spouse when it comes to school issues. Share report cards, notify him or her of special meetings, and

make sure he or she is included in all important placement decisions.

47. Parent Advocate

Find an advocate who will come with you to parent-
teacher conferences or other school meetings. This individual can help you view problems less emotionally
and more objectively. An advocate can be a friend with
expertise in schooling issues or someone who is especially trained in parent advocacy.

48. Mom Likes You Best

Don't compare your kids! Don't even think the com-
parisons, much less say them out loud. Find the unique
strengths and talents of each child, and stop trying to
make one child measure up to another.

49. Baby-Sitter Blues

Whether you have a live-in nanny, an occasional baby-
sitter, or out-of-home child-care arrangements, be sensitive to the possibility of problems in this area that
may be surfacing as school stress. One family I know
recently discovered that their live-in nanny was using disturbingly harsh and punitive disciplinary tac-
tics for their three active sons. Once uncovered and
dealt with, their children's school lives improved
dramatically.

50. Classroom Interventions

Ask your child's teacher to permit some modifications
in expectations until your child is back to normal in

his or her attitudes and attendance at school. Some possibilities include, but are not limited to:

☐ Reducing the amount of homework initially to achieve small increments of success, and then gradually increasing expectations as confidence increases.

☐ Having frequent, even if short, one-to-one homework conferences with the student to assess completion rate, quality of work, and problems he or she may be having.

☐ Developing a homework buddy system in which the buddies monitor each other to make sure assignments are understood and all necessary materials are taken home. Encourage buddies to exchange telephone numbers.

Consistency and predictability in a classroom are especially helpful to anxious, over-conscientious children who are constantly in doubt about whether they're doing the right thing. Teachers might:

☐ Develop a classroom/subject matter reference book that contains frequently used vocabulary or spelling words, rules, procedures, checklists, and mathematical formulas.

☐ Develop specific and consistent classroom routines to facilitate learning and organization (for example, how to get help when a student has questions, where to turn in completed assignments, or what to do when free time is available).

5

What to Do If the School Won't Help

I remember a time when our dinner conversations were no longer happy and lighthearted. Usually I would talk about the interesting things that had happened during my day as an elementary school principal—the student who brought a dead frog in a bottle to class, or the deer that wandered onto our playground from a nearby forest preserve. My daughter would talk about letters she'd received from one of her dozens of pen pals. My husband would talk about the rise and fall of the Dow Jones. And Patrick, our sixth grader, would talk about everything under the sun. But lately his conversations had focused on only one topic: his teacher. He told horror stories of her gloomy moods and bad tempers. He recounted the number of students reduced to tears by her vicious attacks. He never seemed to be the object of Mrs. McCray's vitriolic tongue; he merely observed her with fear and trembling, wondering when she would turn on him. We tried the approach that many parents take when confronted by a school problem: we told him to ignore it and it would go away.

But every night at dinner and bedtime the worries and complaints would pour forth. After several weeks, I decided to check out his story with a number of parents I knew whose students were in the class. I suspected that Patrick had an overactive imagination and things were not really as bad as he described them. My research revealed that, unfortunately, his version of classroom events was depressingly accurate. Sharon's mother said that Mrs. McCray had driven her daughter to tears over a lost homework assignment only that day. Matt's mom quizzed him while I hung on the line. "Yes," she reported, "Matt says the same thing. Mrs. McCray even whacked someone over the head with a rolled up newspaper today." I discovered that the situation was even worse than Patrick had described it.

The next morning I called the school principal and told him how unhappy we all were. I asked him what could be done. Fortunately he was a reasonable person. He didn't argue and tell me I didn't know what I was talking about. Neither did he defend the teacher and her actions. He simply asked me what I would like to see happen in this situation. Patrick and I talked it over. He thought he'd like to transfer out of the class. It meant leaving some of his best friends, but even friends couldn't compensate for seven more months of Mrs. McCray. We made such a move and finished the year without incident. Not every administrator is willing to make changes. Not every problem can be solved so easily. There are times when a more radical change is needed, such as a totally different schooling choice.

How do you know if your child needs a change? How can you tell whether the problem is one your child will have in any school setting or is specific to his or her present classroom or school? Many parents have the philosophy that adversity builds character, and no matter how bad the teacher or the school is, their child will learn to live with it. That's what I call the "teacher is always right" syndrome. On the other hand, some parents react to their children's every whim and are subject to their clever manipulation. That's called the "child is always right" syndrome. Each case is unique and must be solved differently for a child to learn and grow. Before you think about changing your child's schooling, however, let's look at some reasons for having him or her stay put.

When Should You Stay?

Even if you encounter a serious problem in your child's school setting, there are some very good reasons to stay right where you are.

Stay where you are when everyone agrees on the problem and is willing to work on a solution. As wise as we often think we are, we sometimes don't know a good thing when we see it. Before you rush off into some unknown situation, give all the players a chance to work on a solution to the problem. If you're having a problem with a teacher and she agrees to make some changes, give her a chance. If the administrator or school board is responsive, be gracious and admit that you were premature in your judgments.

Stay where you are when you think the problem is your child's and he needs to take care of it, not run away from it. If the problem is your child's, then moving to a new setting will not solve the problem. Moving will only confirm for your child that if he doesn't want to "shape up" or conform, the answer is to simply complain, and Super Parent will come to the rescue. Sometimes children need a fresh start, but give them every opportunity to solve the problem where it started. They will feel better about themselves if they can.

In general, stay where you are if it's close to the end of the school year. Everyone tends to get tired and discouraged after nearly nine months of hard work. Talk about the decision over the summer when life is less pressured. The situation may not look so bleak after you take a step back from it.

Stay where you are until you've had a chance to sleep on it for a week or two, pray about it, and talk it over with several people whose judgment you trust. Only if your child's life is in danger does the decision to change a school need to be made overnight. Give yourself the benefit of time before you make a decision to move.

Stay where you are if it appears that your child is manipulating the situation to get what he or she wants without a sincere desire to change. Some children are masters of manipulation. They know that if they can convince their parents that the problem belongs to someone else, they won't have to "face the music."

Stay where you are when you're in the middle of a family crisis. Making a decision about schooling for your child in such a situation is a big mistake. There might not even be a schooling crisis once the family problem is resolved. Be careful to determine if schooling is really the problem or if some other issue is masquerading as a schooling problem. Often a pastor or family counselor can help you see the situation more clearly.

When Should You Leave?

Having listed the many reasons to keep your child in a particular school setting, we now turn to some very good reasons to pull your child out of a particular school setting.

Transfer when your child is constantly harassed, bullied, or in danger. The problem of playground bullies exists everywhere, but if teachers and administrators will not face up to the problem and deal with it, you as a parent are powerless to change things. You can teach your child strategies for dealing with bullies, but without effective adult support, his life will be miserable if he has become a victim. Children who have different values, who are sensitive, or who are gifted are often singled out for verbal—if not physical—abuse.

Transfer when your child has become involved with the wrong peer group. Your child's friends will become

more important to her with each passing year of
school. If your child has friends that you feel are influ-
encing her to act in unacceptable ways, then do everything in your power to get your child away from those
friends. Be reasonable in your judgments, however. My
children have had many friends with strange clothing,
weird hairdos, unusual lifestyles, and bizarre tastes in
music and reading, but that doesn't necessarily make
them a bad influence on my child. If, however, you can
document a decline in your child's motivation, attitudes, respect for family rules, and moral standards,
that is genuine cause for alarm.

*Transfer when your child is regularly being exposed
to drugs, sex, or violence.* If your child has to worry
about drugs, sex, and violence as part of his daily environment, he will have little time to concentrate on
learning. And neither will anyone else.

*Transfer when your child is failing with no hope of
rescue.* No child should fail in school. There's no reason
for it. Find a place where he or she can get the kind of
help and attention that is needed. Tackle problems like
this very early. High school failure, unless it is sudden
or isolated to a class or two, did not begin in high
school. It probably began in first grade. Pay attention
when your child begins to get failing grades. Something serious is wrong—either with the child, with the
teacher, with the parents, or with the school. Find out
what the problem is and get help.

*Transfer when you object to virtually everything the
school does.* If you are constantly ready to criticize
every decision the school makes and find fault with

every word the school issues, then leave. Your children will be much happier if they don't constantly have to worry about your reaction to every little thing that happens in school. You need to be able to trust that school personnel have the best interests of your child in mind. If you can't do that, you're better off in another setting.

Transfer when you have an unresolved conflict with the school administrators or teachers. Children know when the people who are important in their lives aren't getting along. They suffer when their parents disagree over things, and they also suffer when their parents and teachers don't agree. You must be able to wholeheartedly support your schools.

There are some exceptions to this rule. At the high-school level my children have had teachers whose methods and/or character I questioned. My children and I discussed the issues, and at that point in their lives they were able to deal with the situations as adults. I let my children know that disagreeing with their teachers' methods or lifestyles, however, didn't give them an excuse to do poorly in class. I expected them to continue to do their best. At that point I knew they could do it.

Transfer when the teachers are inadequate and no one will do anything about it. There are inferior teachers everywhere. Some of them are very nice people—they just can't teach. If your child gets one of those teachers and there's nothing you can do to get your child into another classroom, look for another school. Nothing should stand in the way of your child's learning. That is why she is in school. There's too much to accomplish to waste a year in an unproductive situation.

Transfer when your child is not achieving to his or her potential because of a lack of programs and services. If your child has a special need and no one will address that need, find another school.

What about Unresponsive Administrators?

Even in the best of school districts, there are still some administrators who were trained to believe that parents should be seen and not heard. They are resentful and defensive when confronted with knowledgeable and assertive parents, and they can make positive problem-solving in the school setting very difficult. Faced with an individual like this, you will need to strategize and plan very carefully to get problems solved productively. Being highly visible in the school environment is one way to ensure that an unresponsive administrator will take you seriously. There are dozens of ways you can increase your visibility at school (even if you work full-time).

Meet

Arrange for at least one informal conference a year to chat about what is happening at school, your child's progress in his or her classroom, and any other issues you have on your agenda. This conference should have no real purpose other than to establish a good working relationship with the administrator. Follow up your visit with a brief thank-you note of appreciation for the time the administrator devoted to talking with you.

Volunteer
If you can't volunteer at school on a regular basis, perhaps you can make instructional materials at home or talk about your job during a career day. By all means join and become active in the parent-teacher organization at either the school level, the district level, or both. If you can only be at school occasionally, volunteer to help with class parties or field trips whenever you have the opportunity.

Every positive exposure you have to the school and its personnel is "money in the bank" when it comes time to deal with an unresponsive administrator. The unresponsive administrator respects and understands political influence and power, and through your involvement you're sending the message that you know how to use power. Naturally, throughout all of your school involvement you're working to develop trust with all school personnel by keeping your promises, being punctual, being thorough and conscientious, and dealing with problems rationally rather than emotionally.

When teachers and administrators—for one reason or another—behave in an unprofessional manner, these situations are far less likely to involve children whose parents are positively visible at school than to involve children whose parents are extremely negative or who are totally uninvolved.

Go Higher Up

Finally, when faced with an administrator who refuses
to offer any help whatsoever on a school problem, the
option of contacting his or her superior and ultimately
carrying the problem to the school board always exists.
But there is a price to pay for escalating the problem to
this level. You will lose any credibility and support in
the local school if you do so. Even teachers who know
you are right in what you are doing may circle the
wagons and defend their fellow educators.

What Can I Do about Incompetent Teachers?

You'll seldom get your child's principal to admit that
he or she has an incompetent teacher on staff. But as
was mentioned earlier, the fact remains that some
teachers are much better than others, and some are
downright harmful to your child's emotional health.

The most important thing you can do in this area is
to discover through your own personal research who
the best teachers in your child's school are and then do
everything in your power to make sure your child gets
assigned to one of those teachers. Each school works a
bit differently with regard to class assignments. Once
you've figured out how the game is played in your school
you will know how to strategize to get what you want.

The worst thing to do (and I discovered this from
personal experience) is to wait until the class list has
been posted or school has started and then demand a
change. The administrator in this situation will be

loathe to change a decision that has already been made since this would make him or her appear to have "given in" to pushy parents. Instead, find out when teacher assignments are made, and make an appointment to see the principal well in advance of that time. The best strategy focuses on the positive aspects of one classroom teacher and the educational needs of your child, rather than making negative statements about a specific teacher or veiled threats about what you will do if you don't get your way. Put your teacher request in the form of a letter that details your thinking and offers supporting data. If the teacher is truly incompetent, you will probably get what you want if you plan ahead and act in a rational manner.

What Can I Do about Tracking?

Another issue of importance with regard to student placement involves *tracking,* sometimes called *grouping.* Tracking is the placement of students in classes on the basis of their ability. This practice often begins as early as first or second grade. The unfortunate part of tracking is that once a student is assigned to a "low" group, or track, he or she rarely moves out of it.

The idea of tracking is based on some assumptions that at first seem quite logical and sensible. After all, don't children learn better if they learn with those who have similar abilities? Won't children who learn more slowly be embarrassed and suffer emotional and educational damage if they are placed with brighter classmates? Don't teachers and administrators, with their years of training and experience, know what is best for students with regard to class placement? And can't teachers do a better job of teaching if all of the students in a particular group they are instructing are on a similar level? The answers to these questions is not necessarily yes.

Your efforts to minimize or abolish low-ability tracking should focus on gathering good information. The following questions should be discussed in public forums: How does the school make tracking decisions? How are teachers assigned? How many classes are tracked? How may children assigned to low tracks ever move into higher ones? What is the distribution of track enrollments according to children's race and gender?

6

Activities to Build Confidence and Independence for School Success

One of your main goals as a parent should be to raise a confident and independent child. This goal cannot be achieved overnight or simply by doing something positive occasionally. There are, however, many parenting practices that, if carried on consistently during your child's formative years, will contribute to his or her becoming a confident and independent child.

Confident and independent children handle stress, frustration, and failure with aplomb, not anxiety. Confident and independent children deal with defeat by picking themselves up and trying again. Confident and independent children *will* encounter school stress—there are no guarantees against that. But they will be able to handle it more effectively. Confident and independent children have learned to be resilient and adaptive.

The following activities will help your child develop confidence and independence.

Talking to Yourself

I don't know about you, but when I'm in a difficult situation, I talk to myself. Sometimes I even do it out loud. I have a litany of statements I reel through that have helped me in the past. "Now, don't panic, Elaine. There's a solution to this problem. Maybe it doesn't seem evident at the moment, but we'll figure out a way. You'll only make the situation worse if you panic." And so it goes. Help your children learn to talk themselves through difficult situations, "thinking out loud" as they go. Of course, the self-talk should always be positive. "I can do it. It doesn't matter if I made a mistake. I'll do better next time."

Talking to God

My own elementary school career was pretty stressful. I moved to a new school when I was ten and I didn't fit in at all. I dressed differently, actually liked to study, and always got picked last for playground games. I spent a lot of time on the outside looking in. I handled a great deal of my school stress by talking to God. For some reason it never occurred to me that my parents would be interested in my problems. They seemed to have enough of their own. But God was there, so I talked to him nonstop about the unfairness of it all. I knew he was listening, and talking to him made me feel better. I survived the rocky beginning of my education and even made a couple of friends, but if God hadn't been there for me, I'm not sure I would have made it. Encourage your children to pray, and pray with them every night.

The Three *P*s and Other Pitfalls

*P*rocrastination, *P*erfectionism, and *P*oor prioritization are the biggest bugaboos of kids with school stress. They don't manage their time well, yet they want whatever they do to be perfect. So they wait until the last minute and then end up tearing through a ream of paper, making mistakes and starting over. Teaching your child to plan ahead, to break large jobs into small, manageable pieces, and to set reasonable goals for the finished product will be lifelong challenges, but if you don't start early, you—and they—will be sorry.

Take a Deep Breath

If kids could learn to stop in the middle of a bad situation, take a deep breath, and count to ten, parents and teachers would certainly lead more relaxed lives. Teach your kids to take their own "time outs" when they feel themselves getting out of control.

Problem-Solving Skills

The confident and independent child has good problem-solving skills. Teach your child to use the following
steps whenever he or she has a problem. Soon the
process of solving problems will become second nature.
(Younger children will need the simplified version
given after this.)

Step One: Begin to define the problem. Talk it over
with a trusted friend or adult and write it down.

Step Two: Gather information. Get input from all of
the people involved in the problem.

Step Three: Redefine the problem. The problem may
be worse than you thought and have several aspects
to it, or you may discover you really don't have a
problem at all.

Step Four: Establish an acceptable outcome. Decide
what you want to have happen as a result of solving
the problem, and, if at all possible, make the outcome measurable.

Step Five: Generate alternatives. Don't just settle
for one solution to the problem; your first solution
may not work.

Step Six: Establish the plan. Make sure you explain
why the plan is being prepared, who is going to

participate, what specific actions each individual will take, when these activities will be performed, and where they will occur.

A simpler plan that is more appropriate for younger children consists of the following steps:

Step One: Stop! What is the problem I am having?
Step Two: What are some plans I could use?
Step Three: What is the best plan I could use?
Step Four: Do the plan.
Step Five: Did my plan work?

Nutrition and Diet

In our frantic world, fast food and microwave dinners are becoming a regular part of our lifestyles. Your child needs a balanced, nutritious diet to meet the demands of school. The highly processed foods crammed with additives and empty calories that comprise the primary diet of many kids is enough to make them sick (literally). Too much caffeine and sugar can also exacerbate school stress in addition to putting your child at risk for chronic infections. Teaching your children about the connection between what they eat and how they act and feel is an important part of raising confident and independent children.

Fit as a Fiddle

I cringe when I hear of school districts cutting their

physical education budgets. Children who are physically fit are better learners. In my school we did fitness training on a weekly basis, entered our students in the Presidential Physical Fitness Competition, and monitored the height and weight of all of our students. If your children don't have the benefits of a comprehensive physical education program at school, make sure you build fitness exercises into your routine at home. Here are just a few of the benefits of exercise: it increases circulation; strengthens muscles, bones, and ligaments; reduces fatigue; relaxes nerves; evens out emotions; and increases resistance to disease.

Empathizing with Your Child's Point of View

Your child will face problems with less frustration and more confidence knowing she has parents who can empathize and understand her point of view. Empathizing doesn't mean always agreeing with your child, but it does mean being able to listen and understand where she's coming from.

Breaking a Big Challenge into Small Pieces

When your child is faced with a big job (for example, cleaning his room, doing a school research project, or building a model airplane), teach him how to break it up into small steps and pieces and to concentrate on finishing one step before worrying about the next one. Once mastered (and it will take much modeling, practice, and reinforcement), this lifetime skill will help your child face seemingly insurmountable tasks with calm and confidence.

Write a Contract

If your child sometimes has problems following through on promises or responsibilities, try establishing a contract with him or her. Prepare a document setting forth your mutual responsibilities in carrying out a plan, then sign it and have your child sign it. You can write behavior contracts, academic contracts, and home-chore contracts, among others.

You're Special!

Help your child find and develop her own area of expertise. Whether it's drums, violin, basketball, calligraphy, public speaking, raising rabbits, or collecting stamps, support and encourage your child's unique interests and talents.

Copy Cats

Face it. Your kids are going to pay more attention to what you do than to what you say. Remember to behave in a competent, mature manner so that when your kids do copy you, you'll be happy with what you see them doing.

Self-Defense and Emergency Preparedness

Your child will feel more confident and safer in potentially threatening situations if he or she has had some training in self-defense. My son, Patrick, experienced a marked improvement in his confidence level after he enrolled in karate classes. I've seen the same thing happen to other young people who experience the discipline and rigor of martial arts. The training doesn't make young people more physically aggressive or intimidating. Rather, it gives them a quiet confidence in their own abilities to defend themselves if they should need to.

Also take the time to train your children about what to do in different kinds of emergencies (at home, at school, on the playground). Talk about how to get help from an adult when needed and how to use the telephone to call 911 for help in an emergency.

I Can Do It by Myself

Be ready to let go of your children when they reach a new level of maturity. You don't have to force them or push them to new stages of independence, but neither should you hold them back. As your children grow, the physical distance between you and them may grow larger and the separations may grow longer. But keep your fears in check and understand that this newfound independence is an integral part of your children's maturity. Otherwise you may be guilty of tying your children to your apron strings.

Learn From Your Mistakes

One of my favorite TV commercials shows basketball great Michael Jordan detailing his many failures. The punch line of the commercial has Michael explaining to viewers that without experiencing failure he would not have been motivated to achieve greatness. Help your children look upon their mistakes as learning experiences. One of the benefits of sports and other kinds of competition is that they teach children how to pick themselves up after a failure and do better the next time.

MYOB

Teach your child how to "mind your own business." This is an important social skill that can help your child stay out of trouble in the classroom, on the playground, and in life. Don't interrupt. Don't eavesdrop. Keep secrets and confidences. Don't get mixed up in somebody else's arguments. Stay on the bench when a fight breaks out. At least half of the discipline problems in a school would disappear if kids would learn this simple lesson.

Money Wise and Responsible

Being able to earn and manage money is the hallmark of an independent and confident child or young adult. Teach your child how to be a good employee and then how to manage the money she makes. Help your child learn how to be a valued employee by giving her responsibilities at home and encouraging her to find odd jobs in the neighborhood.

Learning Can Be Fun

Play learning games at your house whenever you get the chance. Whether the games are the kind you buy in a store or ones you make up, if you show your child that learning is fun, he'll be on his way to becoming a confident and independent child. Turn family trips into learning experiences and make shopping excursions hands-on lessons. Learn something new every day. Turn your home into a learning center by making sure you have reference materials, lots of books and magazines, games and educational toys, and plenty of "stuff" with which to build and make things, do experiments, and complete projects.

Facts on File

Knowledge is power. Knowledge also creates independence and confidence. Teach your children as many facts and as much information as they're willing to soak up. Memorize poetry, the Gettysburg Address, and the Preamble to the Constitution. Learn the Ten Commandments and the Beatitudes by heart. Even if your child attends a private or public school, you should still be "homeschooling," which means taking every opportunity you can to make learning at your house fun.

Don't Be Afraid to Ask

Knowing when you need help to do a task or find your way, as well as knowing how to ask for it, are characteristics of confident and independent children. Teach your child how to ask for directions, how to use the reference department of the library to get help with difficult questions, and how to ask a classmate or a teacher for homework help. We always feel more confident if we know where we can turn when things get tough.

Up Front

Speaking in front of a group is one of the most feared and stressful activities for most people. If you can help your child overcome his fear of speaking in front of the class, you'll have given him a real boost in confidence.

An annual event at the elementary school where I was principal was Biography Day. Each fifth-grade student chose a famous historical figure, researched his or her life, and then prepared a short speech assuming the role of the famous person. Dressed in creative and often elaborate costumes, the students stood in front of the entire school and their families and gave their speech from memory. I was always thrilled when 100 percent of our students were able to do this very complex and difficult assignment. I always provided support, coaching, and encouragement for those who were especially nervous, and I promised to be right in the front row to prompt them if they forgot. But they never did. Every child needs to have an early and successful experience with public speaking to build confidence.

Thank You Very Much

Learn how to give and accept compliments, and then teach this important social skill to your children. Being able to graciously say thank you when someone says something nice to you is a skill that many people find difficult. But being able to do it is the mark of a confident person.

Home Sweet Home

Make sure your children know that no matter what happens to them out in the "cold, cruel world," home is a safe place where parents and other family members will help them regroup and try again.

Develop a family motto or mission statement that will unify your family and focus your efforts on positive goals. "We Care," "Energy and Excellence," and "Family First" are examples of mottos some families have chosen.

Safety First!

Children who have been indoctrinated with the rules of safety will always feel more secure and independent than those who haven't. Teaching safety begins the minute your infant starts moving around independently and ends when your kids leave home to live on their own. Don't leave the important safety lessons to chance or to someone else. Arm your children with safety information and rules.

Who's Calling, Please?

My first impressions of children I haven't met are often formed when they answer a telephone call I make. I can tell a lot about parents and their children from a brief telephone exchange. Give your child a script to follow and spend time rehearsing with him before you permit him to answer the phone on his own. After he's passed the telephone-answering course, begin teaching him how to make telephone calls to seek out information for you. How to look up numbers in the book, how to find the telephone number of someone who isn't in the phone book, and how to make simple phone calls to find out when a movie starts or whether a store has something in stock are all confidence-builders for a child.

Kids Are People, Too

Demonstrate by example that you believe that kids are people, too. Show your children that you respect their individuality, that their ideas are worthwhile, and that their feelings are valid.

In the Olden Days

Tell your child about your own experiences growing up.

Give her examples of how you overcame adversity or succeeded after failing; how you were teased and lived to tell about it; or how you compensated for a disability. Read aloud inspirational stories to your child that feature real people accomplishing amazing feats. Ask grandparents, aunts, and uncles to tell their stories so that your child will have a sense of your family history.

Friends Are Friends Forever

Encourage your child to invite friends over to your home. Get to know your child's friends and include them in your family circle. I consider my children's friends to be mine, and I share my friends with them.

The Family Support Network

Extended families are a luxury in today's highly mobile and transient society. I grew up with loads of cousins, aunts, uncles, and grandparents close by. They were always there when I needed them, and some of them still are. Our holidays were filled with large gatherings, good food, and laughter. My own children were not so fortunate. Their family circle was much smaller and more distant. But we still maintained the same philosophy: *We're here for you whenever you need us. Just call!*

Walk a Mile

As far as I'm concerned, walking has got to be one of

the best activities ever discovered. It cures ills and ailments, helps us lose weight and keep fit, enables us to enjoy the beauty of nature, gives us time to talk and share with family and friends, and is a guaranteed way to reduce stress. The benefits are endless! Start walking daily with your children. You will be amazed at the positive effects. Keep track of your mileage, and when you reach important milestones (fifty or one hundred miles, for example), celebrate with a party.

Teamwork

Give yourself a gold star if during the past twenty-four hours you worked on a project or a task with your child. Perhaps you cooked a meal, cleaned out the garage, raked leaves, or pulled weeds. You don't get the star if you assigned the chore and then went on to do something else on your own. Nor do you get the star if you started out working together with your child and then threw up your hands in impatience and said, "Run along and play. I can finish this." Allow your child to experience the satisfaction of working side-by-side with an adult and receiving a pat on the back for a job well done (or done at all).

Live on the Wild Side

Take a risk. Go out on a limb. Do something different. Surprise your kids. Plan a weekend getaway and don't tell the kids until they get up on Saturday morning where the family is headed.

The Test Drive

It's one thing to let your kids go. It's another thing to let them take your $20,000 automobile with them. But sooner or later, we have to trust our kids. It's easier to accept the major separations that come later if you've gradually released the fledglings from the nest when they were younger. We let our daughter, Emily, take the car to drive on busy suburban Chicago expressways only days after she got her driver's license. She managed to get lost, but we learned the importance of taking test drives ahead of time to build confidence and independence. Ever after we "rehearsed" new destinations.

How Much Is That Doggy in the Window?

There's nothing better than a pet to help a lonely and clingy child gain self-esteem and confidence. Pets build responsibility, relieve stress, and provide companionship. And if your pet is one that needs exercise, the daily walks will be an added benefit. If you have yet to find a hypoallergenic cat, and a dog is too much work right now, settle for hamsters (that unfortunately sleep every human waking hour) or fish (as long as the kids know they don't cuddle well).

Life Skills

Teach your child as many life skills as you can. Cooking,

doing laundry, changing a flat tire, washing windows, CPR, first aid, hanging a picture, or wallpapering a room are just some of the many valuable skills you could teach. If you know how to do something, pass along the skill to your child. When your child comes through in the clutch to take care of himself or others, he'll be the star of the show.

Be a Sport

I love to visit our kids and grandchildren in Michigan. They keep us on the move during our entire visit. Our son has run in several marathons and our daughter-in-law runs six miles a day just for fun. Their four kids think nothing of a six- or seven-mile walk or a fifteen-mile bike ride. When I discovered that our ten-year-old granddaughter had accompanied her father on his final twenty-six-mile practice run for the Chicago Marathon (she rode her bicycle), without complaining, I was delighted. I can't say for certain, but perhaps the children's physically fit bodies have something to do with their honor-roll grades. Make sure your children know how to swim and play some team or individual sports. One doesn't have to be super-coordinated or play in the pros to realize the confidence-building advantages of sports.

Computer Whiz

Being technologically literate builds confidence in kids by giving them a head start in their personal lives, at school, and on the job. If you can afford it, buy a computer. Besides building confidence, it's likely to improve your child's grades.

Antidisestablishmentarianism

Teach your child big words. Have fun with them. Learn to spell them, say them, and use them in conversation. A good vocabulary will help your child's reading and writing skills.

Find Your Way

While you're chauffeuring your daughter from school to lessons or to shopping, take some time to teach her the names of streets, directions, and alternate ways to get from Point A to Point B. When she gets good, let her tell you the street names and which direction to turn. This activity builds awareness of a child's surroundings and is an impressive skill for any child to have.

Raising confident and independent children is getting more difficult in today's dangerous world. But it can be done. If you're eager to have more hands-on information that is relevant to your neighborhood and community, identify three or four high schoolers in your area who are achievers. Ask their parents how they managed to raise confident and independent kids. You'll find out it wasn't easy. There were bumps, breakdowns, and many detours on the road. But you'll be encouraged by the stories they tell and energized in your own quest to guide your child.

Endnotes

Chapter 1: Why Do Kids Refuse to Go?

1. I. Berg, K. Nichols, and C. Pritchard, "School Phobia and Its Relationship to Dependency," *Journal of Psychology and Psychiatry* 10: 123-41.

2. L. A. Hersov, "School Refusal," *Child Psychiatry: Modern Approaches,* M. Rutter & L. A. Hersov, eds. (Oxford, U.K.: Blackwell, 1977).

3. Phillip W. Jackson, *Life in Classrooms* (New York: Holt, Rinehart and Winston, 1968) 10.

4. I. Berg, "When Truants and School Refusers Grow Up," *British Journal of Psychiatry* 141 (1982): 208-210; and I. Berg and A. Jackson. "Teenage School Refusers Grow Up: A Follow-Up Study of 168 Subjects Ten Years on Average After In-Patient Treatment," *British Journal of Psychiatry* 147 (1985): 366-370.

5. A. R. Brulle, T. C. McIntyre, and J. S. Mills, "School Phobia: Its Educational Implications," *Elementary School Guidance and Counseling* 20 (1985): 19-28; and J. E. McDonald and G. Shepard, "School Phobia: An Overview," *Journal of School Psychology* 14 (1976): 291-306.

6. R. A. Moss, "The Role of Learning History in Current Sickrole Behavior and Assertion," *Behavior Research and Therapy* 24 (1986): 681-683.

7. Brulle, et al. "School Phobia: It's Educational Implications" 19-28.

8. K. Oahara, "Prevention and Treatment of Childhood Suicide," *Japanese Journal of Child and Adolescent Psychiatry* 28.2 (1987): 86-90. M. F. Shaughnessy and M. B. Nystul, "Preventing the Greatest Loss—Suicide," *Creative Child and Adult Quarterly* 10 (1985): 232-238.

9. McDonald and Shepard, "School Phobia: An Overview" 291-306.

10. G. Perugi, J. Deltito, A. Soriani, and L. Musetti, "Relationships Between Panic Disorders and Separation Anxiety with School Phobia," *Comprehensive Psychiatry,* 29.2 (1988): 98-107.

11. P. Adams, "Psychoneurosis," *Basic Handbook of Child Psychiatry* ed. J. D. Noshpitz, vol. 2 (New York: Basic Books, 1979) 194-235.

Chapter 2: What's Behind Your Child's School Stress?

1. Alexander Thomas and Stella Chess, *Temperament and Development* (New York: Brunner/Mazel Publishers, 1977) 22-23.

2. Thomas Holmes and Richard Rahe, "Holmes-Rahe Social Readjustment Rating Scale," *Journal of Psychosomatic Research,* vol. 2 (New York: Pergamon Press, 1967).

3. Gerald Herzfeld and Robin Powell, *Coping for Kids: A Complete Stress-Control Program for Students 8-18* (West Nyack, N.Y.: The Center for Applied Research in Education, 1987).

4. R. S. Weinstein and S. E. Middlestadt, "Student Perceptions of Teacher Interactions with Male High and Low Achievers," *Journal of Educational Psychology* 71: 421-431.

Chapter 3: Getting Them Back to School

1. B. Levinson, "Understanding the Child with School Phobia," *Exceptional Child* (1962): 393-398.

Chapter 4: Fifty Fabulous Ways to Reduce School Stress

1. Thomas Phelan, *1-2-3 Magic: Training Your Preschoolers and Preteens To Do What You Want* book and videocassette (Carol Stream, Ill.: Child Management, 1990).

2. Dorothy Rich, *Megaskills: How Families Can Help Children Succeed in School and Beyond* (Boston: Houghton Mifflin Company, 1988).

3. Thomas Armstrong, *In Their Own Way: Discovering and Encouraging Your Child's Personal Learning Style* (New York: St. Martin's Press, 1987).

More Shaw books by Elaine K. McEwan

Angry Parents, Failing Schools: What's Wrong with the Public Schools and What You Can Do About It (0-87788-019-0)

Managing Attention and Learning Disorders: A Guide for Adults (0-87788-181-2)

The Guide for Parents and Educators Series

The ABCs of School Success (0-87788-635-0)

Attention Deficit Disorder (0-87788-056-5)

Solving School Problems (0-87788-640-7)

The Practical Tools for Parents Series

"The Dog Ate It": Conquering Homework Hassles (0-87788-389-0)

"I Didn't Do It": Coping with Dishonesty in Children (0-87788-177-4)

"Mom, He Hit Me": What to Do About Sibling Rivalry (0-87788-556-7)

"Nobody Likes Me": Helping Your Child Make Friends (0-87788-590-7)

Available from your local bookstore or from Shaw Publishers.